Philip Parry & Glenn

# PHILIP P

# &

# Glenn Pye

# Taxi Tales

Philip Parry & Glenn Pye Taxi Tales

Copyright Philip Parry 2012

# Also by Philip Parry

## Wishful Thinking

Set in the 90's, this is the story of a young, unemployed man living in a small town on the outskirts of Liverpool. Unbeknown to him, he is granted three wishes. Through the monotony of daily life he first innocently wishes for some excitement, and very soon this wish is granted. Unfortunately, excitement comes in many forms, and his life soon dramatically changes. The story, language, and characters are very real, with humour, sadness, love, emotion and horror. "Wishful Thinking" is simply the story of an average man, and his thoughts and wishes. So remember... be careful what you wish for!

## View from My Mind

This is the first two of Philip's 'View From My Mind' series of poetry books in One paperback version. The poetry has been created from childhood through to the present day. Philip touches on religion, love and society in general and uses his own emotional state at the time of writing to bring the poems to life.

## About the Authors

I was born in Harwarden Grove, Seaforth, Liverpool in 1966. I lived there until I was 8yrs old. At that time my parents decided to emigrate, and took me and my 2 brothers and 2 sisters to start a new life in New Zealand. We lasted only 3 months as the feeling of 'homesickness' set in and simply took over. On returning I had a brief spell living in Bootle Merseyside with my very 'streetwise' uncle. The family was split at that time, some in Bootle, some in Skelmersdale, living with an Aunt. After picking up some 'tips' from my uncle and his friends 'Oddjob' and 'Tinker', we eventually all moved to a house in the then new town of Skelmersdale. This is where I still live. Poetry, writing and photography are all passionate 'hobbies' of mine, and in my poetry I simply try to express my own feelings and thoughts. To me, a poems 'meaning' is decided solely by the 'reader' and therefore should be read with an open mind.

Glenn, was born in Melbourne, Australia, to the parents of ten pound poms. He moved over to England in the mid seventies and after a short time living in Liverpool, he moved to Skelmersdale and has lived there since. Glenn along with myself, became a taxi driver around the same time and through the job is where we met. Since I had Wishful thinking published, Glenn has created my blog and web pages and also became interested in the writing side of things. Together we have created Taxi Tales which is also available in e-book format.

## Author's Note

These tales are all actual events that have happened to either me or Glenn. I have worked as a taxi driver for twenty three years now and Glenn for twenty four. As you will have gathered, between us we have an awful lot of experience and have been involved in many many different situations and met a whole variety of people. After reading all of the Taxi Tales you will realise that we both work in a small town so don't have the typical 'guess who I picked up today' stories from drivers that pick famous people up. We pick 'you' up, the general public. None of these tales would have been possible without you so we thank you all, good or bad, for being the real 'stars' of this book.

We have not and never will mention any of your names, but believe us, WE KNOW WHO YOU ARE!!!

## Contents

# Sunday Bloody Sunday-The Hold Up

I had been out working in the morning and had gone home for my lunch, My wife asked me not to go back out to work but spend some time with her instead. Although I was very tempted to have the afternoon off, I told her that I still needed £23 to finish off my radio settle. (Settle is taxi terminology for rent of the equipment used i.e. Taxi radio, meter etc) I told her as soon as I have made this money, I would finish for the day. This turned into one of those decisions in life you regret.

I had done one local job when I was sent to pick up a fare going to Liverpool. I was given a house address to pick up from but my fare was already standing on the road when I pulled into the estate. He was in his early twenties and about 5 foot 10 inches tall, just an average looking guy. He climbed into the back of my car with his sports bag, and told me he was going to Liverpool Airport.

The journey from Skelmersdale to Liverpool Airport normally takes about half an hour, so I was quite glad that this guy was very chatty. We talked about normal stuff, sports, weather etc, and he told me he was off to Dublin for a few days to see some family. We got onto Speke Boulevard, which is about two miles from the airport. He told me that he had four hours until he had to be at the airport and he's going to pop in to see a friend in Aigburth, which is about five miles from the airport. He gave me directions to where he wanted me to go, turn left here, right there, until we ended up in a little court yard and the journey came to an end, and my nightmare began.

7

As I put on my hand brake I felt two dull thuds to the back off my head, I instantly turned around to find a gun pointing in my face. I could see the white rubber mallet he had used to hit me with in his other hand. He started to scream at me to give him my money. I can remember just looking at him, it seemed like minutes but it would have only been seconds. I had a feeling of 'is this really happening? I knew it was but just couldn't believe it. He screamed for the money again. I passed over my money clip which had my wallet stuffed into the top, he grabbed it and put it into his sports bag and at the same time put the white rubber mallet into his bag as well. He shouted at me "GIVE ME YOUR FUCKING WALLET!!!!!!!!!"

"You've got my wallet" I replied, but this fell on deaf ears.

"IF YOU DON'T GIVE ME YOUR FUCKING WALLET I'LL FUCKING KILL YOU, YOU PRICK!!!!!"

At that point he pressed the gun into my head, and screamed again" I'M NOT FUCKING MESSING AROUND.... GIVE ME YOUR FUCKING WALLET OR YOU'RE FUCKING DEAD!!!!!!!!!!!!!!!!!"

At this point I screamed back "IT'S IN YOUR BAG... I GAVE IT TO YOU WITH THE MONEY CLIP!!!!!"

He looked at me with such hatred in his eyes, he was so angry he started to open his bag.

"If you're fucking lying I'm going to fucking shoot you, you fucking gobshite," he said.

He looked in the bag and found the wallet, "Yer it's fucking here, you're fucking lucky, now give me your keys"

You've  seen the films were the actor is trying to put keys into the ignition and they fumble and drop the keys, their hands shaking so they can't do an everyday simple task, well that's what I was like in reverse. It seemed an age to get the keys out of the ignition, which wasn't making my new 'best mate 'any happier.

He screamed once again "GIVE ME YOUR FUCKING KEYS DICKHEAD!!!!!!!!!!!!!!!"

I managed to get the keys and pass them to him, he took them off me, looked at them for a few seconds, and then passed them back to me.

"You can keep them," he said, then opened the door. He then turned to me and said, "Don't fucking move from here for five minutes. If you do, I'll find out where you live and I'll fucking kill you. Got that dickhead?"

I just nodded, anything to get this guy out of my car. He opened the door got out, then put his head back into the car.

"Remember dickhead, five minutes!" he reminded me.

He slammed the door and walked around the back of the car and just stood there. I was watching him in my rear view mirror, I couldn't just drive off as I needed to reverse to get out of the court yard, and he was now blocking the way. Why I didn't just reverse over the top of him I still do not know! Then to my horror he walked back to the car and opened the rear door behind me. At this point I thought he was going to kill me. Panic set in. I could feel my heart beating faster, I turned around in my seat to face him, but he wasn't looking at me he was looking at the glove compartment.

"Open your glove box," he said, but in a calm voice.

I leaned over and opened it and he looked at the contents, which was just some CD's and paperwork.

"Alright, remember five minutes or I'll find you and fucking kill you. Got it!" he said.

"Ok," I replied, and with that, he closed the door and ran off.

All this happened in about five minutes but it seemed a lot longer than that, as every second was like living in slow motion.

Well his five minutes, and mine, I don't think were the same. About thirty seconds after he disappeared from view I once again was living in a Hollywood film and took an age to get the keys into the ignition. I reversed the car, and headed out of the court yard. While doing this I picked up my microphone and tried to get into contact with my office. I told the operator at my office what had just happened, (well I screamed it to him), he was asking where I was. By this time I was back onto the main road, were I pulled over and told him the name of the street. He rang the police and told me to stay where I was, I just sat there again for what seemed like an age, but in reality was about five minutes before the police arrived.

The first police car on the scene came over to me and asked were the robbery had taken place. I told him the direction because I didn't know the name of the road. Just then, the armed response unit turned up. The police man who I was talking to told the armed response unit were it took place and they sped off towards the court yard. The police man looked at my head, it was cut a little and had a big lump on it from the hammer. He rang for an ambulance to take me to Liverpool Royal Hospital and by this time one of the drivers from my firm had pulled up. God knows how he got there that fast. The police asked me to sit in his car because mine was now a crime scene and he told me that they would be taking it away for forensic testing.

I got into the taxi, while I waited for the ambulance and I just sat there. The driver asked how I was…. it was then I burst into tears. I don't care if people think that because I'm a man that I shouldn't cry, fuck that macho crap. Looking back I have to feel sorry for the driver sitting there with me crying.

The ambulance turned up and the paramedic had a look at my head, and told me that I would have to have an x-ray to see if my skull was fractured. He told me that the skin was broken but I didn't need any stitches, which was a bit of good news. They put me in the back of the ambulance and took me to the accident and emergency department and once inside the hospital I was seen straight away. The doctor asked me several questions, trying to find out if I had concussion. He then told me that I didn't need an x-ray. At this point a policeman came into the room, sat down on the chair opposite me and waited for the doctor to finish with me. A nurse came into the room to take my blood pressure, while the doctor was telling me the signs for concussion, and that if I get any of these signs I would have to go straight back to hospital. The nurse had finished taking my blood pressure, she turned around to the doctor who was still talking to me about what I should look out for, and said to him," His blood pressure is very high doctor," he looked at her if she had just landed here from a different planet, and said," It's hardly surprising given what he has just been through." Well, we all burst out laughing.

The policeman asked several questions about the man's description, height, weight, hair colour etc, and asked for a brief account of what happened. He told me that I would have to make a formal statement but that it could wait for a few days.

After receiving some pain killers for a head ache, I got discharged from hospital and the taxi driver from my firm took me home. I have never been so relieved to be home. Two days later I returned to Liverpool to pick my car up and to make a full statement, one thing that struck me as bizarre when making my statement was that the policewoman who was taking it asked at the very end, "Did you give this person permission to take your property?" I think the look on my face said it all, "I have to ask" she said.

I returned to work after about three weeks, still to this day I get nervous about lads sitting behind me, but you have to get on with it, you can't let these bastards get the better of you. Some people when asking what happened, asked if the gun was real, can you just imagine the scenario,

"GIVE ME YOUR FUCKING MONEY!!!!!!!!!!!!"

What was I was supposed to reply?

"Before I part with my hard earned money is that gun real or is it a fake?"

The other thing people asked was," Why you didn't you just snatch the gun off him?" Jackie Chan has a lot answer for!

Some people asked, "Why didn't you run him over when he was standing at the back of the car?"

Well, the simple reason is I froze, this wasn't Hollywood, and I'm not Bruce fucking Willis. This was real life and until you're in that situation you can't say how you're going to react.

The police never caught this guy; well I hope he enjoyed the £37......... Yes you read that right.... THIRTY SEVEN POUNDS!!!!!!!!!!!!!!!......... that he took from me. Not a lot of money for what I went through.

Anyway, that's Glenn's story.

While Glenn relived this nightmare story to me, I could see from his expressions that this has left a lasting mental scar. I take my hat off to him for his handling of this memory and the fact that he has continued to work as a taxi driver...... I seriously believe that if this had happened to me I would certainly never have driven a stranger anywhere ever again.

I personally hope the man that committed this cowardly act, reads this story, as his face is etched clearly in Glenn's memory!!!!!!!!!!!!!!!!

Just a reminder........ All the Taxi Tales are true!!!!!!!!!!!!!!!!!!!!!!!!!! Phil.

# Wanker

About ten thirty one night I was waiting to pick up a fare outside a pub in Up Holland. Wigan had been playing rugby that night against St. Helens and many of the people I had already picked up were rugby fans. After about five minutes waiting, three huge men came out of the pub. They looked more like rugby players than fans, and all were extremely tanked up.

Two of them got into the back, both were in their mid twenties, the third man that got into the front was older, about forty.

The two men in the back were loud and singing what I assumed were rugby songs. The man in the front told me to just ignore them, and told me they were going to Billinge.

I started driving and after about half a mile, the man in the back left suddenly announced that he wanted a wank.

"What did you say you fuckin' queer?" his mate asked.

"I said, I want a wank. Is that ok with you?" he replied.

"Don't care what you do you fuckin' queer," his mate said.

"Well I fuckin' do!" I pointed out, still thinking that this was obviously something he'd decided to say thinking it would be funny because he was drunk.

"If I want to have a fuckin' wank I'll have a fuckin' wank!" he told me.

"Not in this car you won't mate!" I said, now thinking he was going to start being more stupid and cause trouble. This thought filled me with a certain amount of dread as one of them alone would have been more than a handful, but three!!!!!

The man was quiet and I assumed he had understood that I meant what I had said.

The journey continued quietly for a few moments and I stupidly believed it would continue that way. How wrong I was!

Suddenly the man's friend started shouting.

"YOU FUCKIN' DIRTY FUCKIN' BASTARD! PACK IT IN YOU FUCKIN' DIRTY FUCKIN' QUEER TWAT!!!!!!!!!!"

The other man was laughing hysterically.

"Oh calm down I'm only having a wank, what's up with that?" he said whilst still laughing.

My heart sank and my blood suddenly boiled. I glanced over my shoulder and to my horror seen that he was indeed, having a wank!

The size of the three men became suddenly and totally no worry to me as I had one thing in mind. The 'wanker' was getting out of my car whether he, or his two friends, liked it or not.

I slammed my foot onto the brake pedal and the car screeched to a sudden halt. I unclipped my seat belt and twisted round in my seat to face the man, who was looking shocked but still with dick in hand.

"Get the fuck out of my car now!" I said as calmly as I could.

He didn't move, just stared at me.

"I said, get the fuck out of my fuckin' car!" I said again but louder and through gritted teeth.

Still, the man didn't move.

"Right you dirty bastard, get out or believe me I'll get you out!" I explained, and meant every word.

"No, fuck off!" he said, staring at me and smirking.

That was now enough for me, and not thinking of any consequences or having any real plan of action, I went towards him trying to land several punches about him as I attempted to get into the rear of the car. He pushed himself backwards to get out of range of my fists and started shouting.

"OK OK OK YOU FUCKIN' NUTTER!" he squealed.

The man in the front suddenly grabbed me and pulled me away, I was still throwing punches towards the man but was now being restrained completely.

"OK OK MATE STOP! I'LL GET THE IDIOT OUT!" he said.

"WELL FUCKIN' DO IT THEN, RIGHT NOW OR I'LL FUCKIN' KILL THE DIRTY BASTARD!" I yelled.

He opened his door and got out and yanked open the rear door.

"Get out!" he told him.

The man paused, looked at me staring at him, looked at the older man, and then slowly got out of the car.

The older man calmly shut the rear door and climbed back into the front seat. As soon as the door shut I drove on. The journey lasted another five minutes or so and all that time the two remaining men kept apologizing for their friends' behaviour.

I was still too angry to even speak.

I got to the end of the journey and told them the price. The older man in the front payed me and then gave me a substantial tip and again the both men apologised.

"It's ok, it's not your fault, it's that dick head mate of yours," I told them.

"Well we're sorry mate anyway," the younger of them said.

"Ok mate cheers, see you later then," I said, and turned the car and headed back towards Skem.

I could not stop thinking about what the man had done and I was still so angry that I decided that if I saw him on my way back I'd stop and have words, well, maybe more than words!

I rounded a bend and readied myself to soon stop as it was not far from here that he got out.

My angry thoughts suddenly stopped and were replaced by elation. There he was, in the exact same spot I'd left him, standing with his hands covering his exposed manhood, and a Police patrol car was parked on the road in front of him. The two Officers, both female, were stood in front of the man. I burst into laughter, and realised that beating him up would have been much less satisfying than this. I couldn't resist slowing down as I passed in the hope that he saw me, and he did. As he looked at me I calmly displayed the 'wanker' sign with my hand to him out of my window. I only wish I had a camera as his face was an absolute picture!!!!!!!!

'Right then, next please,' I thought, and continued with my working night

# Who's In My Office?

One afternoon I was sent to a local factory, and told to wait at the offices and main reception. I parked outside and after a couple of minutes a man approached. He was tall, confident looking and wearing what looked like an expensive suit. He was carrying a briefcase and talking loudly on his mobile phone. He opened the back door, threw his briefcase onto the back seat, slammed the door shut, and then got in the front passenger seat.

"Hello, is it Manchester Airport you're going?" I asked.

He grunted. I assumed this meant 'yes', and started to drive. After a mile or so, he dialed a number on his phone and then began telling somebody to 'do this' and 'do that', in a tone that was clear to me that he was used to people doing exactly what 'he' said.

He then stopped talking and looked at me, and in the same rather unpleasant tone he said, "Turn that down!" and looked towards the car radio.

The radio was not playing loudly, and because of his assumption that I would do this for him, I simply, didn't.

He spoke more orders down the phone then again he looked at me, and in a louder and more aggressive voice he said, "Turn that down!"

Again I simply didn't.

He then said with clear agitation in his voice down the phone, "Right, I'll have to phone you back, I cannot hear a thing!" and ended the call.

Then he looked at me and said with a scowl, "I told you to turn that down, twice!" and glared at me.

I glanced at him and said calmly and clearly, "Yes you did, but in case you haven't noticed, you are in MY office now, not yours!"

He looked as though he had just been chastised by his mother, and from that moment on, he did not speak another word, and strangely, did not make another phone call!!!!!!!!!!!!!!!!!!!!!!!!!!!!!!!!!!!!!!

# The Runner

A runner is somebody who runs off without paying, (as you can see, my profession put a lot of thought into this terminology). As you know we taxi drivers, are famous for our aptitude.

I had only been driving a taxi for about three weeks when one Saturday night, about three in the morning, I got a pick up at an address in the old part of town. I pulled up outside the address and watched as the front door opened. A young lad came out of the door and stood on the step, he then started to give his girlfriend a goodnight kiss. The time this took them made me think that the lad was going off to war. Anyway, he eventually dragged himself away from her and got into my car. He told me his destination which was to the new part of the town. I tried to speak to him but he didn't seem to want to talk, which was alright, some people do some don't. As I pulled into his road I asked where he wanted to be dropped off, he replied, "Just here."

Before I could even tell how much he owed me, he opened the door and was off running down an alleyway. He ran that fast he could have given Hussein Bolt a run for his money. Golden rule is to never leave your car unattended, but I didn't have to go after him as I had the address where he came from. Some people are even outwitted by Taxi Drivers!!!!!!!!!!!!.

So I just drove back to the house where I picked him up to ask his girlfriend for the money, or at least the lad's home address. I pulled up outside the house, it was in total darkness, but I wanted my money, so I knocked on the door. I stood there for about thirty seconds, no answer, so

I knocked again but this time a lot louder. Then the upstairs bedroom window opened. A man's head popped out, looked at my car, then back at me, and shouted "I HAVEN'T ORDERED A F***ING TAXI!" and was about to close the window.

"No, no, no..." I stuttered... "I picked up here about twenty minutes ago and the lad I picked up has done a runner"

"WAIT THERE!" he ordered..... I obeyed!

As I waited, I began to question whether this was in actual fact a good idea. The downstairs living room light came on and I took a couple of steps back, I was a fresh-faced 21yr old at the time, the man looked to be about 40. The front door suddenly swung open, and he stood looking at me. He was dressed in an old T-shirt and his boxer shorts and looked distinctly vexed, to say the least!

"Say that again!" he said. I explained that I had picked up a young lad from this house and told him where the lad had gone, what he looked like, and more importantly the fact that he had not paid.

He then turned round and bellowed up the stairs, "SHARON!!!!!!!!! GET DOWN HERE NOW!!!!!!"

After a couple of tense minutes, Sharon appeared in her dressing gown. Sharon was the lad's girlfriend and the extremely angry man's daughter.

"Do you know who this is?" the man barked at her.

"Erm...no," Sharon replied.

"This is the fucking taxi driver that picked your dick head of a boyfriend up. Well, your dick head boyfriend ran off and didn't pay!"

Whilst this was going on, I was stood watching and listening and had an overwhelming feeling of 'Uh oh!!'

The man asked me what I was owed, I told him it was £2.20. He went inside and returned with £3 and told me to keep the change.

As I turned and began to walk away I heard him telling Sharon that he was going to fucking kill that little dick head when he sees him next.

Me, being the young and rather cheeky 21yr old, said, "Hey mate, is there any chance I can come back and watch you kill him?"

He looked at me, and for a split second I swear a smile flickered across his face, and then he growled, "FUCK OFF YOU PRICK!", and confirmed to me that he wasn't actually smiling.

I took his advice and, shall we say, I rather hastily left!

To this day I still don't know if the 'dick head' is actually still alive!!!!!

# Angelina's Mother

On a very busy Saturday night I got a job to pick up at a nightclub in Wigan. This particular club is well known for its rock nights where all the heavy rockers flocked. I pulled up and parked opposite the club, watched and waited for my fare to arrive. I noticed four massive blokes walk out the exit of the club.

'God these guys are big,' I thought.

They had big bushy beards, and leather jackets on. They were Hells Angels. I even looked for their motorbikes up and down the road. Then to my horror they started to cross the road.

'Shit!', I thought,' I hope they're not for me'.

I decided to do my ostrich impersonation, turned my head the other way and hope these gorillas don't see me or my big car with taxi stickers all over it.

There was a knock on the passenger door window, I slowly turned my head to find the street had been completely blocked by the man's huge frame.  I put my window down and he told me his name.

'Oh god it was the right name', I thought, and so in these guys got.

As every one of these guys got in they all said, "Hello" or "Evening", one even said, "I hope we haven't kept you waiting long"

"No", I replied, and to be honest even if they had I wouldn't have told them.

They all asked me how my night had been, I had a picture on my dash of my two little daughters and they asked about them. As each one got out they said goodnight to their friends as well as me, they were genuinely nice blokes, who just happen to look very scary. But they were a pleasure to have in my car.

My next pick up was in Wigan again, so off I went. It took me about fifteen minutes to get there and it was about four in the morning when I got to my pick up point.

As I pulled up I saw a smartly dressed couple standing there, they both got in the back, and the doors got the 'slammed shut' treatment that they had become used to.

I turned around and asked what their name was to make sure I'd got the right customer, there was still a lot of people milling around so I had to make sure.

"Trust me you're for us", the woman said.

Great start, I've just had the Jolly Green Giant and his mates in my car, no problems at all, now I've got Brad and Fucking Angelina, with a massive attitude.

"What's your name?" I asked again, the bloke gave me the correct name, but I had already named them Brad and Angelina in my mind. I asked them were they were going and the bloke told me.

About two hundred yards into the journey, Angelina started, "Where have you been, we've been waiting for you for about forty minutes, so where have you fucking been?"

One thing I've learnt over the years is when someone is pissed up and angry, it's no good shouting back, the situation just gets worse, so I tried to pacify her.

"Sorry I'm late but it's always a bit busy at this time, everyone wants a taxi at the same time, but you're in the cab now so I'll just get you home"

"I'm not interested in other fucking people I'm only interested in me, so were the fuck have you been?" she screeched, "Forty minutes I've waited for you, so come on tell me", she continued.

'Bollocks trying to pacify her', I thought.

"Right,.." I started, "... I've only had the job fifteen minutes, so I've not kept you waiting. So if you've got a problem ring the manager on Monday, because I don't need to listen to this"

"You're here so you will fucking listen" Brad piped up.

His timing with that comment was brilliant, I was about twenty yards from a bus stop, and she was starting another volley of abuse. I pulled into the bus stop.

"What are you doing?" Brad asked.

"Get out", I said.

"You can't kick us out, I'll get you the sack", Angelina shouted.

"For one, I'm self employed so good luck with getting me the sack and two, I have the right to refuse custom. Now get out", I told her.

Brad could now see the situation getting out of control.

"Look mate were sorry for having a go at you but we need to get home, we've got a babysitter there, so could you please just take us", he said.

"Ok", I said "But not another word or there won't be a second chance, just sit back, be quiet, and I'll get you home", I explained.

"Ok, no problems mate" Brad replied.

So off we went with still about six miles to go. We hardly got six yards before Angelina started again.

"I think you're fucking disgusting threatening to kick us out when we've got a baby at home", she moaned.

"Listen love, when I pulled over to kick you out I didn't know you had children, it was only when your husband explained that you needed to get back for the kids that I decided to take you, and I hate to point out the fact if you were that worried about your kids you wouldn't be out till three in the morning", I told her.

"Don't fucking tell me how to run my life you cheeky bastard", Angelina said, clearly now losing her temper completely.

"Who the fuck are you to talk to me like that?"

I pulled over again and turned to Brad.

"Listen mate, you're not paying me enough to put up with this, could you please tell her to be quiet or the next time I pull over you're both out, kids and babysitter or not. Oh, and we are now out of the town centre so the chances of you getting a taxi here at this time of night is nil", I explained.

"Alright mate, just carry on", he said quickly.

That seemed to do the trick and there was not another word from Angelina all the way to their home. When we pulled up outside their house, Angelina gave the door another huge slam, and marched into her house.

"Can you take the babysitter home?" Brad asked.

"Yer no problem", I replied.

We worked out a price which included taking the babysitter home and he gave a twenty pound note and told me to keep the change. I couldn't believe he was giving me a tip.

"Sorry about what happened mate, I'll send the babysitter straight out, thanks for bringing us home", he said.

"No problem mate", I said.

I sat and waited for about five minutes before the babysitter came out.

'Oh God', I thought.

Out from the house walked a battle axe, whom I assumed to be Angelina's Mother.

She had an 'I take no shit from anyone look' etched into her weather worn face.

She looked like the kind of middle age woman who could have easily taken on the four giants I picked up earlier if they had attacked her, and not broken into a sweat.

She got into the seat next to me, and I took a deep breath and readied myself.

"Hiya love, you alright?" I asked waiting for my head to be chewed off.

"Yer not bad. I believe you had words with them two", she said.

'Oh no here we go, I think I'll write my will out now, she's going to kill me', I thought.

"Yer, we had one or two words", I gulped.

"Yer my son in law said you were going to kick them out, and I bet it was all that mouthy bitches fault", she said.

I burst out laughing.

"You know her well then?" I asked.

"I should do, I'm her mother!" she answered, and laughed.

For the rest of the journey she told me about her grandkids and asked me about my children, and was a very pleasant lady.

Sometimes the apple 'does' fall far from the tree!!!!!!!!!!!!!!!!!!!!!!!!!

# With Some People You Can't Win

One Wednesday afternoon I got a job to pick up at an old person sheltered housing accommodation. I could see on my taxi screen that the lady I was picking up was only going to the local hairdressers, which was situated about two hundred yards from the pickup. As a lot of people living in the sheltered housing are not very good on their pins, I had no problem with this journey. I love picking up the older generation, you get some great stories from them, but to be fair I didn't think the journey would be long enough to get any conversation going.

I pulled up outside the sheltered accommodation, the front door opens and this little old lady aided by two walking sticks starts heading towards my car. I jumped out of my car and said to the lady, "Are you getting in the front or the back?"

She was only about 10 feet away from my car when she waved one of her sticks at me and replied in a very stern voice "Get back in the car, I can manage to get in by myself"

"You sure love?" I asked.

"I've told you once haven't I" she barked at me, giving me a sharp look.

"Ok" I said, and got back into my car. I watched her struggle to open the heavy door, then watched her struggle closing the door as she had to lean half way out to get the handle.

"You going to the hairdressers at the bottom there love?" I asked in my most pleasant voice,

"Yes" she grunted

So I drove to the hairdressers, pulled up outside, she paid me the fare, and then I made the fatal mistake of asking "Are you alright getting out or do you need a hand?"

The look she gave me was enough of an answer and she got out, closed the door and shuffled into the hairdressers.

The following Wednesday I was lucky enough to get the same job, picking up the same lady going to the hairdressers. So off I went and pulled up outside the sheltered accommodation. I sat in my car watching the little old lady, aided by her two walking sticks make her way to my car. She opened the door, leaned half way out to close the door, pretty much the same thing as last week, except when the door was closed she turned to me and said, "Most drivers have the manners to get out and help me into the car, you're a very lazy and unhelpful man."

I just looked at her in disbelief, and before I could say anything she added, "Just drive if you can manage that."

I took a deep breath and drove her to the hairdressers again. As she handed me the money she spat out "Not that you deserve this."

I took the money and started to open my door, "Don't bother yourself I'll manage," she said to me in an angry tone. I chose to get out the car, but she waved me away when I tried to help her, not wanting to get slapped with one of those sticks I stepped to one side, and watched her struggle out of the car. Then watched her shuffle into the hairdressers.

As I drove away to my next job, still bewildered by what just happened, I wondered what she did for a living. School teacher sprung intently into my mind, or maybe a prison officer, or she could have been in the army, but which one I thought, then the penny dropped, I knew what she did, she was probably an SS Officer and has been hiding in England since the end of the war, and that's what I'm sticking too.

But lesson learnt, so next Wednesday I'll make sure I'm not in that area at the time, which for the next three Wednesday's I wasn't however on the fourth. I pressed my button on the taxi screen to except a job and when I looked at the details of where the pickup was I thought 'nooooo', I looked at the customer's name, 'noooooooooo', I thought should I tell the office I've got a flat tyre just to get out of doing this job, but no I decided to do it. As I drove to the sheltered accommodation, I decided on how I was going to handle this. I pulled up outside and watched as the little old lady with her Gestapo boots on shuffled towards the car aided by her walking sticks, I jumped out of my car and was told politely but firmly to get back in my car. I smiled to myself, job done, my plan was to take the first bollocking off her instead of the second one.

# Police, Camera and No Action

My mobile phone rang whilst working, at about 4.45am.

"Hello," I said.

It was the operator in the taxi office.

"Alright Phil, do me a favour, I'm getting' a right ear bashing here. Will you go to the Empire Theatre in Liverpool as quick as you can for me? Them two fella's from Digmoor are down there and already been waiting nearly an hour mate, and they're not happy!"

"Ok, no prob's mate, I'll put my foot down," I replied, knowing exactly to whom he was referring, as it was the same night each week that they went to Liverpool.

The two men were regular fares of ours and were never ever any trouble to any of the drivers. However, they always seemed to be trouble to everybody else and seemed to always end up fighting and causing trouble. Anyway, the journey to reach them would take about thirty minutes, sticking to the speed limits that is. But at this hour of the morning, with what sometimes seemed to be only myself out on the roads, I estimated about fifteen minutes at most.

The journey started, and with no other vehicles in sight I soon reached the end of the motorway and continued along the A-roads. The traffic lights were all in my favour as I shifted speedily along.

Through Aintree, Walton and Everton with no problems, then onto Scotland Road and to the junction of Great Homer Street. The lights again were kind and stayed green, I turned left onto Great homer Street at some speed and with no people or cars in view, I accelerated up the empty road. Then I saw headlights coming towards me, and as I neared I thought the square shape on the roof of the vehicle was a 'Taxi' sign, and took no more notice as I thundered past.

Then, in my mirrors came the sudden illumination of blue flashing Police lights, followed immediately by the now distant squeal of the Police siren.

"Oh for fuck sake! That's all I fuckin' need!" I said aloud.

Thinking quickly I decided not to slow down just yet, and waited for the bend in the road. I then stepped on my brake pedal as I knew the officer 'chasing' me would not now be able to see how long my brake lights were illuminated for, and so therefore, in my mind, he would not be able to calculate my speed.

I slowed quickly and the next lights were red but just before I reached them, the Police 'dog van', streaked past me and then with screeching and smoking tyres, it skidded to a stop across the front of me.

'Here we fuckin' go,' I thought, and readied myself for my forthcoming ticket, and no doubt 'patronising' ticking off!

My window was open half way and the Police Officer got out of his van. The Police Alsatian in the back was barking fiercely and loudly but nowhere near as loud as the Policeman was shouting as he marched towards me.

"TURN OFF THE ENGINE NOW! GET OUT OF THE VEHICLE NOW!" He yelled.

'Holy shit, it's fuckin' Robo Cop,' I thought as he reached my window and then yanked open my door.

"I SAID TURN OFF THE ENGINE!" He yelled again, and the grabbed my car keys and twisted them out of the barrel, stopping my engine.

"GET OUT OF THE VEHICLE NOW!" he ordered, and stood slightly back glaring down at me.

"Ok ok ok, calm down mate," I said as I climbed out.

"GET ONTO THE PAVEMENT NOW!" he yelled.

I walked to the pavement. He walked behind me.

"NOW THEN, I'M GOING TO ASK YOU A SIMPLE QUESTION OK?" he again yelled.

"Yes that's fine, but could you please stop shouting, I can hear just fine mate if you simply speak to me," I pointed out.

He was indeed extremely angry, but seemed to realise that there actually was no need to be yelling.

"Right, what's the speed limit on this road?" he asked.

"I have no idea," I replied.

"What do you mean you have no idea? You're a professional driver and you're telling me you don't know the speed limit on this road?"

"That's exactly what I'm telling you yes."

"Guess it then!" he ordered.

"Ok, I reckon it's fifty then as it is a duel carriageway at the end." I said, knowing full well what the limit was.

"The speed limit is thirty. Thirty miles per hour. THIRTY!!! Did you get that?"

"Yes." I said.

"Now, tell me how fast you were going."

"I don't know." I said.

"Yes you do know, I know too," he said.

"Do you? Well if you already know, why are you asking me?" I asked.

Robo Cops face set sternly and he glared at me intently, took in a deep breath and shook his head slowly.

"I could easily pull the footage from the cameras that are placed all along this road. Do you really want me to do that?" he asked with a smirk.

"Are they 'speed' cameras?" I asked, and also smirked.

"They are CCTV cameras yes," he answered.

"CCTV cameras? Well in that case yes, yes I do want you to pull the footage. That way, when you take me to court, you can show the judge some footage of a taxi passing some cameras, followed by a Police van passing the same cameras. As none of the CCTV cameras will have recorded any speeds, I will be rather interested in the judge's reaction to this utter lack of evidence that you have brought him."

"You where flying is how fast you were going. Flying!" he said slowly.

"How fast is 'flying' exactly? I didn't know my car could go that fast."

"Listen to me, you were going too fast. You appear to be acting like a plank!" he told me.

"A plank? Does that mean stupid?" I asked.

"Yes it does!"

I looked at him and realised by the change in his facial expression and his slightly more rigid stance, that he was now weakening.

"So…" I started, "… is it against the law to be stupid?"

He glared at me, and anger now spread across his face.

"Now you 'are' acting like a fucking plank!" he said slowly.

That was all I needed, and now knew I was not going to get a speeding ticket.

"So let's just clarify something. You are a Police Officer in full uniform including identification numbers that I can clearly see. Firstly you personally insult me by calling me a 'plank' and telling me I am 'stupid. Then you swear at me. This all happening after you have made it quite clear that you have got absolutely no idea what speed I was doing, or in fact 'if' I actually was going too fast. Then let's add on the fact that you have no proof or indeed evidence to back up your 'speeding' claim. It appears to me Officer that it is in actual fact you that is the stupid fucking plank. Oh, and whilst you have been wasting my time here with your pathetic attempt at impersonating a Police Officer that actually knows how to do his job, the two men I was sent to pick up have now probably became so angry that they have either smashed somebody's property, or assaulted an innocent passerby, which actually means that through your actions, a crime or crimes have been, or are being committed. So, I suggest that you give me my keys and I'll continue with my job, and you go and study the rule book some more before you continue with yours."

To my utter astonishment, he handed my keys to me and walked away.

He got to his van then shouted to me, "Just one thing sir,"

"Go on, what?"

"Slow down!" he snapped.

I said nothing and got into my car and decided it was best to let him have the last word.

I finally reached the two men with dread.

'Get ready for this then,' I thought, and braced myself for the expected onslaught of abuse.

To my relief, they simply got into my car and told me where they wanted to go, and both of them fell asleep. The 'slow' drive back was unusually peaceful.

Although I got away with my 'meeting' with Robo Cop without a fine, or in fact being arrested, it was still a frightening experience, but thanks to Robo Cop, not nearly as frightening as my experience with the two men would have been if I had got to them earlier, when they had not become so tired!!!!!!!!!!!!!

# Spiderman

This 'taxi tale' involves a damsel in distress, Spiderman, and myself with the memory of my Father telling me," Men do not hit women!"

One Saturday night/Sunday morning I had just dropped off a fare in Wigan. As I was driving out of the town centre I saw a man and a woman up ahead, they were arguing and the man was pointing in her face. Then suddenly he punched her and she fell. The red stop light I was sitting at changed to green and I sped forwards. The woman had managed to get up and ran across the road, but the man had followed and had stopped her escape and was again shouting and pointing.

I stopped my car and opened the passenger window and began to shout at the man, trying to get his attention from the woman, in the hope she would escape. Unfortunately, my plan didn't really work!!!

The woman ran directly towards me shouting "GET THE POLICE, HELP GET THE POLICE"

I told her to "Get in my car now!!!!!!!!!!"

She did, just as I was about to pull away she screamed "STOP, MY BAG"

I hesitated and she opened the door and pulled in her dropped bag. That's when my heart sank. The man suddenly appeared and pulled the door open wide, I sped off but so did he. He had hold of the door with one hand, both feet inside the car and his other hand was gripping the headrest of the passenger seat.

'Shit' I thought 'just my luck, Spiderman, pissed and out of costume!' I came quickly to a sharp right turn, was in second gear and accelerating. With one thought in my head I heaved my steering wheel and screeched into the road on my right, my thought was simply 'get him off the car' however, he clung on.

I now found myself driving the wrong way down a one way road. Several local taxi's approached me and could clearly see my passenger door open and a madman hanging on to it. None of them attempted any assistance; instead, they flashed their headlights and aimed a variety of angry hand gestures at me. The man then somehow adjusted his position and was able to swing wild punches at me. I pushed the woman forwards and pushed him back with my hand on his chest.

"STOP STOP, WE WILL TALK" the woman yelled suddenly

I pulled over thinking 'good plan' and got ready for him to get off the car, at which point I was going to make good the escape with the woman, and leave Spiderman behind. However, when the car stopped, instead of getting off the car, he managed to get in behind the woman and push her out first, he now had his back to me and his hand on the dashboard, he was short, stocky with a military buzz-cut and heavily tattooed neck.

'Right I thought, here we go' I grabbed him quickly and applied a wrist and shoulder lock as best I could and said as sternly as I could, "Listen dickhead, you hit her because you're a wanker and knew she wouldn't hit you back, try and do that to me and I'll punch you up and down this fucking street ok!!!"

He thought for a moment, then nodded "Ok I'll get out" he said, and to my surprise and relief he did just that. I

39

immediately locked the doors and turned around so I was now facing the correct way.

The man then grabbed the woman by the throat and pushed her into a front garden and slammed her against the house.

"For fuck sake" I thought 'why fucking me?' I stopped and readied myself for the fight and opened my door, just then a police van pulled up next to me.

"Are you ok?" he asked.

"I am but she isn't" I said pointing towards the man and the woman.

"I know, I saw him on your door, wait there I might need you" he ordered, he then parked his van in front of mine and approached the couple.

I sat for a couple of minutes then decided the woman was safe now, and the thought of writing statements and attending court was not something I would have enjoyed, so I drove away.

I was then given another pick up in the town centre. I picked a man up at a nightclub and then had to drive back past where the man, woman and policeman were. It took me five minutes to reach that spot again. When I got there I had to battle with myself to not mount the pavement and run Spiderman and his girlfriend down. The bemused look on the police officers face suggested to me that if I had mounted the pavement and ran them down, that he would have simply turned away!

To my utter astonishment they where hugging and passionately kissing each other. The moral of this story goes something like this: IF PEOPLE WANT TO KILL OR

HURT EACH OTHER...............LEAVE THE SMALL MINDED FUCKING IDIOTS TO IT!!!!!!!!!!!!!!!!!!!!! .

# Fucking Technology

Some years ago when we had all got used to the mobile phone technology, I was thinking how cool I looked with my rather large Nokia handset.

One day I was speaking to another driver, whom, upon noticing my fancy handset (hard not to notice it really, considering its size!) he told me that he had a 'hands-free' kit fitted in his car that would fit my phone, and that he didn't use it so asked if I would like to buy it.

Anyway, to cut this story slightly shorter, I bought it, fitted it inside my car, and proudly placed my Nokia in the cradle.

After two days of making calls simply to tell people that I was actually calling 'hands-free' (most of the people being informed of this were taxi drivers and all seemed mightily impressed!) I picked up a fare in old Skem. He was a tall and rather portly man, with a bald head and was wearing thick rimmed spectacles. I asked him where he was going, and the journey began.

Whilst driving an oncoming car flashed its headlights and the driver waved. It was another taxi driver named Brian. I waved back.

A minute, if that, passed, and my phone began to ring. I glanced at the screen and saw lit up brightly on the display 'BRIAN CALLING'.

I pressed the 'answer call' button, and being aware of how impressed my passenger obviously was, I proudly said," Hello Brian, what's up?"

"Hello, I just wanted to ask you a question Phil," Brian replied, with his voice booming around my car from the secreted hands-free speaker.

"Ask away," I said, and unknowingly falling into the horrible trap that had now been set.

Brian then slowly, clearly, and rather loudly asked this question.....

"Who's that big fat baldy four-eyed wanker sat next to you Phil?"

As my mind worked out the horror of my situation, my hand, like in slow motion, reached out with a finger outstretched, and after what seemed like an eternity, pressed the 'End call' button.

Silence!

The journey continued and I waited for my passenger's reaction with utter dread.

Nothing. Still silence.

We reached his destination, he payed me and I fumbled for his change. As I handed it to him, I looked at him.

He took the change and gave me a rather strange look that I translated roughly into meaning, 'you and your pal Brian are lucky that today I am in no mood for beating the shit out of either of you!'

He got out of the car and walked away.

The next call made was from me to Brian, and the words spoken, only by me, could not possibly be repeated in fear of offending 'any' and probably 'all' of you!

I do think, however, that Brian got the point, although he was laughing whilst listening to my threatening onslaught!

I never again answered another phone call with people in my car. The lesson was most definitely learned!!!!!!!!!!!!!!!!!!!!!!!

# Domestic

The one thing I don't normally get involved in, is customers domestic arguments, which happens quite often, especially after they've had a night on the beer. The main problem is that customers like to include us in their little fights.

Like the couple who, I could see as I pulled up weren't, an advert for marital bliss, as they were screaming at each other on the curb. They got in and both my back doors took the brunt of their argument as they were slammed.

"Evening, where're we off to?" I asked in a cheerful manor

"Take me to my mother's" she demanded

"No, were going home" he shouted at her

"I'm going nowhere with you," she told the love of her life, "I'm going to my mother's," she repeated.

"We're going home!" he screamed.

This went on for a couple of minutes, mums, home, mums, home, until the bloke noticed that we hadn't moved. Then the bloke managed to stop gazing into his wife's eyes and turned to me.

"Are you going to drive or what?" he asked.

Not content with the argument with his wife he now wanted one with me, so I got back into my cheerful mode and told him there's a problem.

"What?" he asked.

"Well I don't know where her mum lives and I don't know where you live," I told him.

"Oh yer," he said, then gave me their address, and I knew what was coming next. Yer you guessed it, she gave me her mum's address, which started the whispering of sweet nothings in each other's ears, sorry... I meant screaming. About five minutes had past since I pulled up and I still hadn't moved an inch, when the bloke leaned over and said, "Listen mate, I'm paying so take me home."

"Sorry love, he wins this round," I told his wife, then I immediately felt some remorse, not for her but my back door. Which I knew was going to get slammed, and she did not let me down when I got her to their house.

Another time I was piggy in the middle, one summer Sunday morning about nine o'clock, I got a job in the old part of Skelmersdale, pulled up outside the house, and a young women came walking to the car, and opened the door, "I've got some stuff that needs going into your boot, could you give us a hand?" she asked.

"Yer no problem" I said.

I went with her to her front door saw a babies Moses basket, and stand, several bin bags full of what I thought were clothes and a few boxes as well as a pram.

'God' I thought, 'This girl needs a removal van not a taxi', but I was here so off I started packing my boot, and most of my back seat as well. I left a bit of space for the customer and baby, assuming that there was a baby somewhere, though I hadn't yet seen one.

As I was about to close my boot I heard a car screech up just behind me, I turned around and a white van had blocked me in, a bloke jumped out of the driver's seat.

"Get that stuff out of your fucking car!" he barked at me.

"No leave it in there!" the woman shouted, as she came down her path.

He completely ignored her.

"Get that stuff out, I won't tell you again!" he ordered.

Now we had a problem, what goes on between the two of them has got nothing to do with me, but now there was a threat to me. I've got her screaming to me "leave it in", and I've got 'Rocky' trying to intimidate me. He came around to the side of my car were I was standing, 'here we go I thought', lovely Sunday morning and I'm going to end up fighting. But once he got to the side of my car he noticed the taxi stickers attached to my door.

"Are you're a taxi mate?"

"No, my fucking car is though," I told him, and just looked at him.

"No, I mean are you on a job here?" he asked, the malice now gone from his voice.

The penny then dropped, she was leaving him for someone else, and this guy thought I was the prime suspect, I fully understood his aggression now.

"Yer I am" I said

"Sorry about that mate, I thought you were someone else," he said

"Yer no problem," I told him thinking, 'this has nothing to do with me.'

The problem was my car was now full and a big white van was blocking my escape route.

He walked around and a big argument started between the two love birds, so I just leaned on the roof of my car, lit a cigarette and watch the argument unfold, along with a few of the neighbours.

After about ten minutes they decided to take it indoors, the lad couldn't apologize enough and took all the stuff back into the house and paid me for my troubles.

Another time I did get involved, and after reading what happened, I hope you will agree that I was fully justified to.

I picked a young couple up from Ormskirk late one Friday night. I didn't see them walk to the car, but boy could I hear them, my poor back door got slung open, the guy popped his head in and gave me his name, unfortunately I was for them. They both got in the back, 'Slam' my poor doors, and set off arguing once again, but at least they told me their destination. So I set off, and just listened to them, or should I say to 'him'. "You're a stupid bitch", "Lazy cow", "Fucking thick", "Your family are nobheads", "You need fucking help"… and so on. You name it he said it to her.

We were about two miles from their destination, when she had just had enough.

"Why don't you just shut the fuck up?" she asked him.

"Who the fuck are you talking to?" he shouted, which to me was a stupid question as she was looking at him and  was in the middle of an argument with him, it wasn't hard to work out.

But the next step shocked me, I heard a thud, then a cry of pain, then silence. I looked around to find the girl holding her nose, blood was pouring out of it and streaming between the fingers of her hand. I slammed on my brakes, which sent the pair of them onto the floor, jumped out of the car and yanked open my back door, (I did say sorry to my back door later!). I then grabbed the lad by the hair and dragged him out of the car. I looked into the car, the girl was now sitting back on the seat, blood still pouring from her nose and crying. I turned and faced the lad.

"Go on hard man do that to me!" I shouted at him.

"Nothing to do with you!" he shouted back.

"It fucking is when it's in my car, so come on dickhead fucking hit me!" I growled.

I leaned into the car and looked at the girl.

"You alright love?" I asked her.

She shook her head, her face was in a right state, blood and mucus dribbling down her chin onto her blouse and her lip was already swelling up. She looked so vulnerable and scared, it was a sad sight.

I turned back to the lad and grabbed him around the throat.

"Go on hit me, or do you just hit women, you fucking shithouse?!" I shouted at him.

This was not like me at all, I'll normally avoid conflict, but this lad was a total wanker and I just wanted to punch his head in. But common sense suddenly kicked in, why should I end up in trouble because of this piece of scum. I pushed him backwards and he landed in some bushes. I turned back to the car, closed the back door, gently, and climbed back into the driver's seat.

I asked the girl her address, she told me, the destination had now changed, the original destination must have been the hero's who was still sitting in the middle of the bushes, legs akimbo! I got the girl to her house, she was still crying and still bleeding. She just sat there.

"Were here love," I told her.

She looked at me, started to cry louder, and after a few minutes she tried to compose herself, she finally managed to speak.

"I haven't got any money, he's got it all," she said shakily.

'Typical,' I thought, 'Trust me to throw the wrong one in the bushes!'

"Listen love you've got enough problems, don't worry about it. Just get yourself inside," I told her.

"Oh, and love?" I said.

She looked up at me, looking worried.

"Do yourself a big favour, fuck that dickhead off, he will do it again, it's your life and you can do what you want, but you're doing yourself no favours being with a dick like him." I said.

"Don't worry I will, thanks for your help, knock around tomorrow for the money ok?" she said.

"Go on get in and look after yourself," I told her.

She got out and I watched as she went into her house.

About six months later I got a job and when I pulled up outside the house I recognised it as the house were this girl lives.

'This should be interesting if she walks out with that prick,' I thought.

But no, she walked out with some other bloke, they both got in the back and closed my doors, gently, and off we went, a couple of minutes into the journey, the girl leaned through the seats and said, "It's you?"

I wasn't going to say anything to her, I didn't want to embarrass her in front of her new boyfriend.

"This is the driver I told about," she said to her boyfriend.

When we stopped at their destination, she gave me a big hug and a kiss on the cheek and her new boyfriend shook my hand. He tried to pay me for both journeys but I refused to take the first payment.

Since then I've picked this couple up a few times over the past few years. They are now married and have a couple of kids!

At last, a happy ending!

# Watch What You're Thinking

I've always had a firm belief that psychics are one of the biggest frauds ever, they play on people's emotions, people that have just lost love ones, telling people that they are going to meet Mr. or Mrs. Right, and  giving people false hope to make a few pounds in the process. I believed that psychics are very good at working things out, asking simple questions and getting their client to tell them the answers without the client realizing, and that was my opinion.

Well that was until one day a lady I picked up changed my mind and scared me half to death  in the process. I picked this particular lady up not too far from where I lived at the time and she got into the front passenger seat. I asked her where she was going, she told me and off we went. I asked her if she was alright, just to break the ice and try and get some conversation going. She gave me a one word answer of "yes", you get a one word answer normally means that the passenger doesn't want to talk when so I just shut up. About one minute later she turned and looked at me.

"Those chest pains you're having are nothing serious, there is no need to worry about them," she said.

I nearly crashed the car, I had been having chest pains for about a week, not bad pains but pains nevertheless, so like everyone else on the planet you think the worse. The thing is I had not told anyone about this, I just looked at her and she gave me a friendly smile. As I said, the pains in my chest weren't too bad, but when she said that I thought I was going to have a heart attack.

"What?" was all I could manage to say.

"Those chest pains your having, there is nothing to worry about," she repeated

All I could do is look at her, and then she said, "You live by railings? I can see railings, like a school, you live by a school don't you?"

I looked at her for a few seconds before answering, "Yes," I stuttered.

"I can see police with plastic bags outside your front door, is your door black?" she asked.

"Yes," I replied

"Don't worry the police aren't there for you" she told me.

'DON'T WORRY? DON'T WORRY?' I thought, any more of this and I 'will' have a heart attack. We were nearly coming to the end of our journey. She turned and looked at me, I was looking straight ahead trying to concentrate on the road, she then turned back looking out of the windscreen. Good I thought, she's finished, but she still had one more thing to tell me. As she looked out of the window she said "Mary is watching over you."

"Who the hell is Mary?" I asked.

"I'm not too sure but she has asked me to tell you this," she replied.

I pulled the car up at her destination, she paid me the fare and got out of my car, but before she closed the door she leaned back in and said "I know you don't believe in this, but what I've told you is true, there is nothing wrong with you, goodbye."

"Bye," I replied, and watched her walk down the path, even when she was out of sight I found myself still looking down the path. After a couple of minutes I drove off and waited for my next job. For the rest of the afternoon I couldn't get my mind off what that woman had told me. But being the sceptic that I was I started to analyse what she said.

The first thing, my chest pains, did I rub my chest when she got in? The answer to that was no. I didn't have any pains in my chest for a few hours. That didn't help me in proving this woman a fraud. Second was where I lived, well I picked her up not too far from the flat I lived in at that time, so she might have seen me there or seen my car parked outside. Third thing was the police, I never seen any outside my flat, never mind loads of plastic carrier bags,... and the last one, who the hell was a Mary?. Well the next day answered a few questions.

The next evening my wife and I were going to my mother's. I had finished work about 5pm, and we left our flat about 7pm. As we walked outside my wife and I both looked at one another, our eyes wide open. The flat opposite to ours had been raided by the police. There must have been about fifteen police men, some by their vans, others by the door of the flat that they were searching, and more were walking from the raided flat to their vans holding plastic bags. My wife, whom I had told about the psychic the night before, and a person who had been to several card readings in the past said, "Do you believe her now?"

I didn't reply, just walked to my car, got in and drove it around to my mum's. Once inside my mum's I began to tell her the tale. She, like me, was not really a believer in psychics, but when I got to the bit about the police raid going on, even she raised an eyebrow. We had a laugh about it and then I suddenly remembered Mary.

"Ever heard of anyone called Mary mum?" I asked.

"Yes" she replied, "My mum was called Mary."

My grandmother died when my mum was only five, she was twenty seven when she died, so she was never spoken about. The last hours events had put a big hole in my fraud theory, so I've come to the conclusion that some people out there actually 'do' have a gift. My wife had great fun giving me stick over the whole episode, turning me from a sceptic to a believer, until I pointed out to her that she has had to pay for her card readings and that not only did I not pay a penny for mine, 'she' in fact had paid me.

# Déjà Vu

This Taxi Tale is a story told to me by one of my customers and as in the last Tale this one is also about thing's that can't be explained. Anyone out there that believes in reincarnation, this tale is for you.

I picked up two women, in their late twenties or early thirties, about three weeks after my experience in 'watch what you're thinking'. They got in my car and asked to go to Wigan. They were off for a girlie night out and were chatting excitedly about what bars and clubs they were going to that night. One of the girls was saying to the other, "Can't wait to get there, we're going to have a few shots tonight."

The girl sitting directly behind me answered, "I don't want to get too drunk tonight. I've got to get up early tomorrow."

"Don't be a bore," her friend said, "...you only live once."

Until she said that I hadn't really spoken to them, just let them get on with their conversation. But when she said you only live once, I piped up, "So they tell us," I commented.

Once I said that, the girl sitting behind me leaned forward between the two front seats and said, "Funny you say that."

"Why?" I asked.

She then proceeded to tell me her little tale.

"Well, two months before I fell pregnant with my son, my father died. When my son was about four years old, I took him to Liverpool to see my auntie, my dad's sister. At the end of my auntie's road is a little park with swings and a slide, so I decided to take my son there before we went to my Aunties house. As we approached the park my son turned to me and said in a very calm voice, "This is where I used to take you when you were a little girl Mum."

Her friend interrupted her by asking, "Did your dad take you there?"

"Yes." she replied.

"Is that the first time you had taken him to see your auntie?" I asked.

Again she replied, "Yes, you know how it is, you tend to lose contact as you get older."

"How did you feel when he said that?" I asked.

"All the hairs on the back of my neck stood up, and it brought tears to my eyes thinking about the time I had spent there with my dad," she said.

"So what are we saying then, there is no need to get drunk tonight because you can do it in your next life?" I asked her.

She laughed and said, "That was the only time he said anything like that and he's never said anything weird since."

I pulled up at their destination, they paid me and as she got out, she said, "There are some weird things in the world that can't be explained aren't there?"

After what happened precisely three weeks earlier, there was only one answer, "Yes!"

Driving back to Skelmersdale, again the sceptical side kicked in. Was she for real? Did that incident with her son really happen? On the drive back I decided that she had no need to make that up, why would she? She told the story, like she'd told it a hundred times before, which she probably has.

So after my psychic friend in 'watch what you're thinking' and this, my scepticism had taken a major knock, and I now believe there are things in this world, even this universe that science or religion can't explain. Thank God, (or whoever or even whatever!!) the next passenger who I picked up that night was a drunk who could hardly talk.

# Fast Food Delivery Service

After a rather hectic couple of hours of picking up extremely drunk and extremely loud and boisterous young men and women, I got a job at a pizza takeaway in Ormskirk. When I pulled up outside, a smartly dressed middle aged man, his wife, and a male friend approached me. The man asked politely if I'd come for them, giving me his name. I was so relieved to be picking up not only polite, but sober and quiet people. As the lady was getting into the back she told me she had a burger, but assured me that she would not eat it or in fact open the container it was in.

The journey began and polite, friendly conversation ensued. I was almost at their destination, a house address, I heard the women say to the male in the back that, "She can't wait to get this burger out of the box," the man giggled childishly, but I didn't think anything untoward at all.

We got to a road and the man in the front directed me to pull up outside a house.

"The one with my BMW on the drive," the woman confirmed, and yes her gleaming new BMW was indeed on the drive. The man in the front paid and they all got out of the car and politely bid me farewell.

After putting my money away, I was ready for my next 'fare' and was given a job to pick up a young girl, just around the corner from where I was. The girl came out of the house after a few minutes and opened the door behind me,

"Excuse me," she said, still standing outside the car.

"There's something on the floor here, I think you better look," she continued.

I turned around and peered behind my seat as best as I could, and could see that she was not joking. I got out of the car and looked properly into the back. I was absolutely infuriated. On the back floor was the last the last women's 'burger'. It was only just recognizable as it had been spread all around the carpet, and wiped across the middle of the back seat, and even had some of the lettuce and tomatoes shoved into the pocket in the back of my seat. I couldn't believe that after being so polite, that this woman had done this, and her 'polite' friend had thought it amusing.

I explained to the young girl what it was and asked her if she would sit in the front for her journey. She said it was fine and was also totally disgusted with what the woman had done. I dropped her off as quickly as I could and drove to the garage nearby. I got some paper towels and some plastic gloves. I had an address in mind that I needed to visit! The night continued after this visit and the car had been thoroughly cleaned.

When I got home I made a cup of tea and wondered what the expression was like on the women's face when she found 'her' burger. Some 'blighter' had pulled the wipers up on her prized BMW, spread her burger all over the window screen, and placed the wipers back. 'Who in earth would do such a terrible thing' I wondered, admittedly with a rather 'smug' look on my face!!!!

# Know Your Limit

I had a pickup one Friday night from Briars Hall in Burscough. I got there about half one and sat waiting for my fare to come out. This happened before we had computerized systems in our cars. Nowadays when we pull up outside any pickup we press a button and the customers' phone rings to let them know we're outside. Back then we beeped our horns and just hoped they heard and would come out. I sat waiting for about ten minutes when finally someone showed an interest in me. A lady walked across to the car, told me her name, I told her I was for her and she turned around to another lady standing at the entrance and said, "Yer it's for us, tell the fella's he's finally arrived," and with that her friend walked back into the pub. 'I'm finally here, cheeky bitch,' I thought, I'd been there for ten minutes, but I was just glad I was picking up to be honest.

After about five minutes, about ten people walked out of the entrance, they all started shaking hands, giving each other kisses, and when they finished shaking and kissing each other, they started all over again. Why is it that when people are drunk they say goodbye like they're fucking emigrating. After about ten minutes of kissing and handshakes and the odd cheeky feel, two couples started to walk towards the car, about five feet away one of the women decided, as she put it 'that she needs to go to the little girls room,' and of course for some bizarre reason women cannot go the toilet on their own. So off trots her friend behind her, which gave license for the blokes to do more handshaking, kissing and cheeky gropes. Finally the two women reappeared, went through the same routine, handshakes, kissing and serious big gropes.

When they got to the car about thirty minutes had gone by since I first pulled up outside, and people wonder why their taxis are late. Two women and a bloke got in the back and the remaining bloke in the front next to me.

"Alright mate," I said to the guy next to me.

"Old Skem," he replied in an extremely blunt manor.

Which tells me that there will be no small talk, just do you job and drive.

"Where about in Old Skem?" I asked.

"I'll tell you when we get there," he said.

'Oh ok then,' I thought, 'Then how the fuck am I suppose to get there if you don't tell me?'

These people think it's a big secret where they live, 'I will find out when I drop you off, just fucking tell me,' I thought.

"Ok," I replied.

The three in the back were chatting amongst themselves, talking about the evening, but happy chops sitting next to me was very quiet, and as we got into Skelmersdale I found out why. Without warning he was sick all over himself, on his seat and the foot well. I pulled the car over.

"What you stopping for, we have to get him home he's not well," happy chops wife said.

"Well now I'm in no hurry, because thanks to him I've got to go home early," I said.

"So, he's not well, just get a move on," she shouted.

"Not well? He's drunk, it's not like he's going to need an operation, he's just drunk, and now more importantly, you do know as well as the fare there is a twenty five pound charge for cleaning that up?" I told her pointing towards the sick.

"I've got the money in the house," she said.

Well that was enough for me, I pulled away from the curb.

"Where are we going?" I asked.

Happy chops wife told me, (I fucking knew I'd find out), when we were about a mile from their home happy chops suddenly said, "You can fuckoff if you think I'm paying twenty five pounds."

I turned to look at him, sick was dripping off his chin onto his nice suit, which was not so nice now as it was covered in sick, I was about to take it back about him being ill, he looked dead but no one had told him yet. He was a walking advert for the anti drinks campaign.

"You are mate, you've cost me four hours work, because you can't handle your ale, all you had to do is ask me to stop," I said.

"One more fucking word out of you and the pair of us will twat you!" His mate from the back piped up. "You're not getting twenty five quid off us and if you carry on you won't get paid at all" he added.

"Is that right?" I asked.

"Yer dickhead, that's right!" happy chops said, while spraying sick all over the place.

I gave him a little smile, picked my microphone up and said my call sign into it, the operator answered me straight away.

"Couldn't do me a favour and send a couple of cars to the corner of Oxford Road, I'm having a bit of trouble with a couple of dickheads?" I asked.

"Yer no problem," he answered, and with that I heard him telling four cars to meet me at Oxford Road. I expected major kick off in the car but to my amazement they didn't hear what I'd done, they were so busy threatening me, they were now in for a shock. Two minutes later I pulled into Oxford Road, to be met by five cars and one pulling in behind me, a couple must of heard what was going on over the radio and decided to go themselves. I stopped the car, turned around and smiled.

"Right dickhead, that's seven pounds for the fare and twenty five pounds for that next to me," I told the bloke in the back. By this time all the other drivers were by my car, I opened my door and explained what had happened, one of the drivers opened the back door and told the bloke to get out, the wives were getting a bit worried, shouting "Please don't hit them!" Funny they didn't say that when their husbands were threatening me. The bloke got out of the back, one of the drivers said your mate is going to have to pay.

"Twenty five quid's a bit steep," I heard him say as I got out of the car.

"Not when he has to go home for the rest of the night, how would you like it if you lost a half days pay because some dickhead couldn't hold his ale?" one of the drivers said.

Another driver said, "Mate no use arguing, that's the price, it's not two against one now, just fucking pay him!"

Happy chops had finally made it out of the car, his wife and the other woman were walking towards their house, the guy from the back put his hands into his pockets and pulled out a ten pound note.

"That's all I've got," he said.

"Well that's twenty two pounds light," I said as I took the money.

We heard a woman's voice.

"It's alright I've got it," happy chops wife was walking back towards us, she headed straight towards me, when she got to me she handed over the twenty five pounds, "Thanks love," I said.

"Sorry about all this," she said.

"Love it wasn't you who threw up or threatened me, just make him suffer in the morning" I said.

"I will!" she said and with that she walked away. Happy chops was walking behind her, but his mate stayed. "Where's my change?" he asked.

I laughed and got back into my car, the other drivers laughed and walked back to their cars, I opened my window.

"Mate, I'm here trying to make a living, your mate has cost me a lot of money, now I have to go home clean his sick up and explain to my wife that we won't be going shopping, but at least your three pound tip has helped," I told him.

I drove out of the street watching him walk away. About three weeks later I got a pickup at one of the local pubs and yes you guessed it, it was happy chops and his mate. They got in the car, both looked at me then to each other, I thought, shit here we go, but no, happy chops was very apologetic and even his mate mumbled an apology. I dropped them off, without incident

# Before You Come Out Of The Closet, Do you Practise Your New Voice

Picked up two young girls and a young 'lad' from Wigan on a Saturday night.  They all got in the back seat and one of the girls told me where they were going.

I started driving and got about a mile into the journey when a song came on the radio. Can't remember exactly what song but the young 'lad' suddenly piped up. In a voice that I can only describe as Liberace like i.e.... camper than a camper van, queer as a bottle of crisps etc etc... and said (almost sang actually) "miiisterrr taaxiii maaaan"

I did not answer him.

Again he sang.... Sorry said, "Miiisterrrrr taaaaaxiiii maaaaaaaan "

Again, I did not answer.

Then, in a louder voice he sang.... Sorry, he said, "MIIISTERRRRRRRRRR TAAAAAAAAAXIIIIIIIII MAAAAAAAN!"

I took a breath, calmed myself down somewhat as I was becoming more well, let's say vexed, each time he used this annoying voice, and said, " Listen mate, if you want to talk to me, in fact if you want me to respond to you when you do talk to me, then will you please talk in your normal voice?"

Silence for a second or two from the back seat, then, "Yoooo waaaanna turn that song uuup don't yooo miiiister taaaaaxiiii maaaaaaaan?" he squeaked.

"No I don't," I replied..."...and I've just told you to talk in your normal voice. Now unless you are prepared to do that then you are wasting your time talking to me because I simply will not answer you." I told him.

Silence then filled the air again until there was a stifled snigger from the girl sat directly behind me.

The young 'lads' response to this was to perform a dramatic yawn, an exaggerated stretch and a flop across the laps of the two girls. They then stroked him and made meaningful comments as to how 'lovely', 'cute', 'quaint' and not forgetting 'adorable' their 'boy' friend is.

The journey ended, with perfect timing as the 'lad woke up just as the car stopped. They payed the fare and all got out in silence and then said their goodbyes to each other and walked away.

I cleared my meter and immediately my next job appeared on the screen in front of me. 'The back of a pub for Mindy'.

I drove the short distance to the car park at the back of the pub and several people where stood waiting for taxis.

A young girl approached my open window and proving to me and anybody else in ear-shot, that she had obviously attended some form of 'finishing school' she said, " Fucking hell, we've been fucking' waitin' here twatting ages so open the fucking door you fucking dick head!"

"However long fucking ages is love, times it by about four and that's how much longer you will have to wait now. Now fuck off away from the car!" I replied, and drove further into the car park.

A voice then sang..... sorry, spoke. It sounded very familiar to me but was coming from a completely different person. It was a young 'lad', wearing what appeared to be his sister's striped tight jumper. He said, "Exxcuuuuse meeee taaaaaxiiii driver, are yooo for Miiiiinndeeeeee?"

'Good God in heaven,' I thought.

"Yes I said.

"WOOOOOOOOOOOOOO" he exclaimed.

He, and his two friends, a girl and a boy, got in. The radio was playing a Take That song as the girl told me the short distance they needed to travel.

Then, to my horror a voice piped up loudly from the back seat and cried," Whooo the fuu*k is this shit on the raaaadio, it's fuuuuuckng shiiiiit! Tuuurn this shiiiiit off riiiight now taaaaaxiiii driverrrrrrrrrrrrrrrr!"

I stopped the car and said, "Get out mate, and get out right now!"

"Arre yooo seeriiiiiuuuusssss?" he shrieked.

"Deadly serious mate. In fact before you consider attempting to question me again I'll give you two choices. Get out yourself, or allow me to assist you out. It will be much better for your health if you choose to get out of your own accord!"

He paused momentarily, then decided. He made the right choice and got out himself!!!!!!!!!!!!!!!!!!!!!!!!!!!!!!!!!!!!!!!!!!!!!!!

# My First and Last Public Performance

When working for Ormskirk taxi's, I was waiting for my turn off the rank and was eventually called to the taxi office. When I got there a lady got into my car and sat behind me.

"Southport please, the Scarisbrick Hotel", she said.

"Ok, no problem," I replied, and began the journey.

The lady sat quietly behind me and the radio played the top ten songs of the time, and then just before the number one song, the DJ ran through the hits just played from 9 to 2. Then after a big build up he announced that the number one song that week was Tracey Chapman singing Fast Car.

By this time I had become quite comfortable with the ladies silence, in fact so comfortable that I had simply forgotten that she was there!

The number one song began, and like many many others it was an absolute favourite of mine. As Tracey began to sing, so too, did I!

I turned up the volume so as to be able to really give it my all, and began to sing loud and enthusiastically. Every word I sang I meant, and every note was hit..... well, in my head anyway!!!!!!!!!!

The song ended, and I felt good. I continued the drive for another mile or so then suddenly remembered the lady, the reason I was heading to Southport, and....... MY SINGING!!!!!!!!!!!!!!

'Shit!' I thought, and took a sneaky glance in my rear view mirror at the woman.

She was sat looking comfortable and thoughtful, and seemingly unfazed.

'Maybe she didn't hear me?' I thought, in an attempt to actually convince myself that my booming voice had not travelled to the back seat of the car.

We arrived at the front of the Hotel.

"Right then love, that's five pounds please," I said, with a tone designed to erase her memory of the earlier performance.

"Ok thanks love, here you go," she replied, and handed me a five pound note.

"Thank you," I said, and was overcome with an 'I've got away with it' feeling.

The back door opened and the lady stepped out of the car. She then stood by my open window, stooped towards me, and handed me another five pound note.

"Oh, erm, what's this?" I asked.

"That my dear, is for the entertainment," she said, and smiled, then walked away.

I could actually feel the heat from my now glowing red face!

# Flashing

This tale has two in one, but all about the same subject, flashing. One night I was sent to Liverpool to pick up a fare. The job was booked for 2am, as I arrived a little bit early, I sat there with my doors locked watching the wonderful sights that happen at that hour in the day. Drunks trying their best to walk in a straight line, women who would have looked immaculate when going out that night now looking like they've been dragged through a hedge. Blokes still trying their best to chat up the girls, while making themselves look like idiots.

As I sat there taking in all the surroundings, I heard someone trying to open my back door, I looked over my shoulder to find two young girls trying the best to figure out why the door isn't opening. I opened my window looked at the girls, they were still trying their best to open my door, one looked and me.

"Your doors broke mate," she slurred out.

"It's not, it's locked" I replied.

"You're not going to make much money like that," the second girl said, then moved from the back door to be level with my door now.

"Are you going to let us in?" the second girl asked.

"Sorry girls I'm booked and I'm going back to Skem," I explained.

The first girl took a step towards me smiled at me and said, "Yer but has your fare got tits like these?"

With that, she lifted her top up and exposed her tits. I smiled back at her.

"I fucking hope so love," I replied.

The two girls laughed and went on their merry way.

My fare turned up about two minutes later, and 'did they have tits like her?'....sadly no! They were four hairy arse blokes!!!!

The second flash tale was when I was taking four girls to Wigan, they were a little bit tipsy, but were just having a laugh, singing to the song on the radio, very poorly, but having fun looking forward to the rest of their night out. One of the girls in the back said to me, "Hey drive, if we show you our tits will you knock some money off the fare?" and the rest of them burst out laughing.

The girl who was sitting in the middle seat in the back said, "look Mr. driver!"

I turned around to see she had her top over her head flashing her tits at me, after several seconds she pulled her top back down, which was a good idea as I hadn't really been looking at the road.

All the girls were laughing and the one in the front said, "I can't believe you did that,"

The flasher replied, "I'm skint, I need to save some money!" they all burst out laughing again.

"Well?" said the flasher, "How much do we get knocked off then Mr. driver?"

I turned around to look at her, smiled and said, "Fuck off love I've seen them now!"

They all burst out laughing, the flasher said, "I didn't think that through really did I? "

They got to their destination still laughing, paid me in full with a good tip and left me with a big smile on my face.

# Please Don't Eat in My Car, It Doesn't Matter Who You Are

Waiting at Wigan train station in the early hours one morning, and watched as my 'fare' approached. She staggered along muttering drunken gibberish and attempting to eat a rather large and greasy burger.

"Are you for me?" she slurred.

"Yes, get in and put that burger back in its wrapper until you get out. Please do not eat it in here." I replied.

Good enough, she then managed to put it back into its polystyrene container and closed the lid.

The journey began, and about a mile into it I asked if she minded me stopping at the petrol station as I was quite low on fuel. She muttered something that I assumed to mean that it was ok with her. I stopped in the garage and began to re-fuel my car, and as I did I glanced inside the car and saw my 'fare' had decided to attempt to eat the burger after all. Extremely, erm, well vexed, I opened the driver's door, reached in and snatched the messy burger out of her hand and dropped it in the bin by the petrol pump. I then closed the door again and finished fuelling, paid, and returned to my car.

My 'fare' was by now more than vexed, she was in fact extremely angry and made no bones about letting me know this. She shouted, swore, called me unimaginable names and seemed to be getting angrier and louder with each word.

"You seriously need to calm down, and you seriously need to stop calling me such vile names!" I told her sternly.

"WHY? WHY SHOULD I? WHAT IF I DON'T STOP EH? She yelled.

"Simple," I said, "If you don't stop, you get out of my car and you walk!"

"WHAT? YOU WOULD THROW ME OUT? GO ON THEN, DO IT! THROW ME OUT THEN!!!!!!!!!!!" she screamed.

"Right then, if that's what you want fine," I said, and slammed the brakes on hard.

The car screeched to a halt, I opened my door, walked around to the other side and pulled open the passenger door.

"OUT!" I shouted.

She stared at me and paused and thought. Then, after she had clearly realized that I was absolutely serious, she climbed out of the car and staggered away.

I watched as she headed off in the total opposite direction, and just then, it began to rain.

I drove away. As we were on an industrial estate I decided to do a lap of the estate and then pick her up again, because I thought the wind and rain may have sobered her up enough to have calmed her down. However, she was nowhere to be seen. I searched for some time then abandoned the industrial estate and decided to go and make sure she had got home safely.

I drove to where she lived, put my key into her door and opened it, walked up the stairs to her room and popped my head inside. There she was, fast asleep in her bed, my daughter!!!!!!!!!!!!!!!!!!!!!!!!!!!!!!!!!!!!!

# Changing Rooms

I got a pickup one evening from one of the local factories. A girl of about twenty five, dressed in her work overalls got in the car, with a couple of bags and a dress in a protective cover, she put the dress over the front passenger seat.

"Evening..." I said, "...where are we off to?"

"Hello..." she replied, "...I'm going to Ormskirk," and told me the name of the restaurant she wanted, she then went on to tell me that she was meeting up with ten friends to celebrate one of their birthdays, then off to Liverpool to see The Chippendales .

"So, straight into the ladies toilets when you get there to get changed?" I asked her.

"No," she replied, and started laughing.

"What are you laughing at?" I asked.

As bold as brass she said, "I'm getting changed in here."

I looked at her in my rear view mirror, she had this big smirk across her face.

"What, you're going to use my car as a changing room?"

"Yep, and I expect you to be a gentleman and not look," she laughed.

"Fuck off, your shit out of luck there, you're going to strip off in my car and not expect me to look, good luck with that," I said and with that, I adjusted my mirror and she burst out laughing, I didn't really think she was serious, but she was.

"I know your wife…" she told me, "…and if you look, I'll tell her!"

"Listen love, when I go in and tell her this story, her first question will be did you look, and if I say no, I was a perfect gentlemen, she would just call me a lying bastard. So I'm going tell her the truth when she asks, I'll say, 'fucking right I did!' I explained.

With this she burst out laughing.

"And remember I am driving, so when we get to the good part tell me to stop!" I pointed out.

"I will…" she giggled, "…but if you do crash, I want to see you explain this to your insurance company!"

I laughed, she was one of those customers that makes the journey go smooth. A pleasant, funny and nice person. Still not thinking she was serious I asked, "So how are you going to do this without me looking? You can't put that dress over your work stuff, because you will get your dress dirty and it won't fit."

About thirty seconds later a pair of jeans landed on the front passenger seat, I looked in my mirror to see her laughing.

"You ready?" She asked, and then takes her top off over her head, leaving her sitting in the back of my car in her bra and knickers. I turned around and she just laughed, I shook my head and turned back around before I smashed my car up.

She started to take her dress out of the protective cover, I glanced at it, it was one of those strapless dresses, so she slips her dress over her head, and about thirty seconds later a bra lands on the front seat resting on top of her other discarded clothes. Then she starts to climb in-between the seat so she can now sit in the front.

"What are you doing?" I asked

"My Makeup now, got a problem...?" she said, "...I haven't got a mirror so I need to use the one in your sun visor."

"Ok," I said.

With that a bag of makeup came out, and she started to put her war paint on. We were about a mile from the restaurant when she had finished, fully transformed from a worker to a party girl.

"I need a favour from` you," she said.

"If you need a hand getting dressed it's a bit late. Go on what is it?"

"I need you to look after my stuff," she said.

"And what the hell am I going to do with it?"

"Give it to your wife in the morning and I'll see her at the school when she drops the kids off."

"Well I'm going to have to tell her now, aren't I?" I said.

"Don't worry I'll tell her you were the perfect gent," she laughed.

"Just tell her the truth, it's much easier," I said, and again she laughed.

We got outside the restaurant, she paid me and went in to enjoy her meal. I finished off my shift, took her clothes home, explained to my wife about the job. She called me a pervert! Seems like it's ok for women to go and see the Chippendales and scream their heads off, but if a girl strips off in 'my' car, yes 'my' car and I look, I'm a pervert!!!!!!!!!!

# The Invisible Taxi Driver

This 'Taxi Tale' is from a driver I worked with when I worked for Ormskirk Taxi's many years ago. He was working late one Friday night and was sent to a nightclub after closing time for one of the staff. The man came out and got into the car. He was one of the 'Door Staff, or 'Bouncers' as they were called once upon a time. He was a huge man with a crew-cut, broken nose, cauliflower ear and a neck like a bull. Oh, and he was not at all amused that his taxi had turned up 20 minutes after the time he had booked it for. He got into the taxi and before his door was even closed he had already called the driver a multitude of rather unpleasant names. The driver was used to this type of abuse and simply waited for the man's tirade to end then said, "Where to then mate?"

The man took a deep breath and said, "Home!"

Where's 'home'?" the driver asked.

"By the Chinese Takeaway on Wigan road," the man said, and glared at the driver.

"Right then, the Chinese it is then," said the driver in as pleasant a tone as he could muster. He began the short drive towards the takeaway and decided it would be best not to attempt to engage the man in any sort of conversation. The man did not speak either, but made a variety of 'huffing' and 'puffing' noises that were clearly meant to show that he was still far from happy.

The journey ended as the driver pulled up outside the Chinese Takeaway.

"That's £1.20 then please," the driver told him.

"How fuckin' much? HOW F**KIN' MUCH? You cheeky little t**t! You're late, then you try and f**kin' rip me off!!!! "The man said as he climbed out of the car. He then walked around the front of the car and stood by the driver's door. The driver rolled down his window and looked up at
the man.

"What do you mean by that eh? I've never ripped anybody off in my life and do not intend to start doing so now. Now why don't you just calm down and pay me what you know you owe me, and stop acting like a fucking idiot?" he said, after deciding that no matter how big the man was, he was not going to be intimidated by him.

The man however, seen things rather differently and decided that the best thing to do now would be to grab the taxi driver through the open window and basically knock the be-jeeesus out of him! He then attempted to do just that, and grabbed the driver by the scruff of his neck and began punching him. After a couple of punches landed on the driver's head, and an almighty amount of struggle and panic, the driver managed to grab hold of the man's jacket and at the same time, put his car into gear.

"FUCK YOU DICK 'ED!!!!!!!!!" he yelled, and holding his jacket as tightly as he could, he began to drive forwards. The huge man had no choice but to be pulled along, trying to stay upright. The car moved faster and as it did, so did the man's awkward sideways steps until at last he lost his grip on the driver and the driver lost his grip of his jacket. The man toppled, the driver continued to drive and as he did, he glanced in his wing mirror and saw the man rolling and sliding along the road. He made good his escape and continued with the rest of his working night, well, that was after a well deserved cigarette.

About a week later the driver was again working and was given an address in Tower Hill road. He found the house and pulled up outside, then, as we all used to do he then 'blasted' the horn. After a couple of minutes, his passenger door opened and a man got in beside him.

"Iya mate…. "He said,"….. where to?"

"The Chelsea Reach please pal." The man answered.

He began the drive to the Chelsea Reach, which was a nightclub in the centre of Ormskirk. As they pulled out of Tower Hill Road the man said," I'm looking for one of your drivers and when I find him I'm going to f**king kill him!"

"Oh yer, and why would that be?" asked the driver.

"Because he dragged me along the side of his f**king car the other night and nearly f**king killed me, that's why!" explained the man.

Until then, the driver had not even looked at the man, but after the penny had dropped, he took a quick glance. The man's face was scraped and bruised badly and his ear was red raw and scabbed.

'Holy shit' the driver thought, and turned his face away from the huge man, and accelerated.

"What? HE DID WHAT? It's unbelievable that a person like that would be allowed to drive a taxi. He sounds like a lunatic. I'll try and find out who he is for you and when I do I'll punch him myself mate. Don't you worry mate, I'll find him and tell you so you can kill the lunatic. We don't need people like that driving taxi's!!!" he ranted, as convincingly as he could, and all the time not facing the huge angry man.

They at last reached the nightclub.

"Right then, that's erm..... £1.20 then please mate.

The man paid with no complaint and said, "Cheers pal, and yer, if you find the little tosser let me know and I'll sort him!"

"Oh believe me I will mate. As soon as I know, you will know."

The man got out of the car and closed the door.

'Thank God for that!' the driver thought as he drove away rather quickly. He then made a large mental note of the address where he had just picked up and from then on, he avoided it like the plague.

# Honest Mate We Just Want To Cross

I have only been a taxi driver for a few months, when late one night, about 3 o'clock in the morning I got sent to Toxteth in Liverpool to pick up fare from a house address. This was years before satellite navigation systems were invented, so we had to use our trusted A to Z maps. As it was dark outside, reading from just the little light in my car wasn't so easy. I found the address and knew which route to take, so I drove down to Toxteth as quickly as possible. If you don't know or have never even heard of Toxteth, It's quite a rough area. Only a few years before there were large scale riots, so it's not a place you want to hang around too long, especially at three in the morning. So before I set off I locked all my doors.

As I was entering Toxteth I could see a group of lads standing by a set of pedestrian traffic lights. As I got nearer to the lights one of the lads pressed the button and when I was about two hundred yards away from the lights when they went onto amber. I looked at the group of lads, counted eight in total, all looking in my direction. Not one of these road safety conscious young men were looking to see if the lights had changed and when I was about one hundred yards from the lights, they changed from amber to red. I looked up and down the road, there was only me on it, the lads were still waiting on the side of the road, still looking in my direction. Now I'm not one to knock anyone from crossing the road safely, but I had a feeling that this particular group of young men were not that concerned about waiting for the little green light telling them it is safe to cross the road, so I decided to drive through the red light.

As I speed past them they all looked at me, and as I looked into my rear view mirror, I noticed not one of them made an attempt to cross the road.

Now for all you people who think I was terrible for not obeying the law and stopping at the red light and letting those young men cross safely, well you'll be pleased to know that because I was so busy looking in my rear view mirror, I missed my turn.

'Easy enough,' I thought, 'I'll take the next left then left again to get to the road I want.' Well it sounded easy enough in my head but I was wrong!

I turned left then started looking for the next left, as luck would have it there was not one for about half a mile, so when I found one I still turned down it hoping to still find the road I wanted. As I turned in I found myself in a square, with a little park in the middle. I drove around the square, which had only one road in and one out and pulled over, picked up my A to Z and began to try and work out a new route. I must have been there for about five minutes, still no closer to finding my way when there was a knock on my window. My head nearly went through the roof I jumped that much!

I turned to see who had nearly given me a heart attack at such a early age, and found a young girl of about twenty years of age bending down looking at me through the window.

I wound down my window and she looked at me and smiled.

"Here for business?" she asked.

Well I don't know how long I just sat there looking at her, but it was a while, that long that she had to repeat her question.

"You here for business?" she asked again, giving me this professional smile.

Now with me being a young twenty two year old lady's man, and realizing she was a prostitute, I shit!

By this time her friend had obviously seen she had picked on a simpleton to ply her trade and walked over, giving me and the car a good look.

I then managed to speak and attempted to say, "Sorry love no I'm lost," actually came out as, "Ssssorry lllove nno iiii'mmm Illlost."

"Oh," she said, and turning to her friend she said, "He's lost."

Her friend walked to the back of my car and saw the taxi plate fitted to my bumper. "He's a taxi driver," she told her friend.

"Where is it you're looking for?" the girl at my window asked.

I picked up the piece of paper I wrote the address onto and passed it to her, both girls could sense I was a bit intimidated by them, but they decided to help me.

"Oh you're not far at all love, just go out of the square, turn left, next left, to the bottom, turn right then it's your first left," she instructed me.

"Ttttthanks," I spluttered.

As she handed me back the piece of paper with the address on it, she put her hand on mine, gave me a big smile and said, "We do a taxi drivers special you know?" then they both burst out laughing and walked away.

I drove out of the square, thinking to myself, 'Well you handled that well you fuckin' tit!' After following their directions, I found the address I was looking for. My fare got in and after the normal pleasantries and telling me were they wanted to be taken, my fare asked, "Did you find it alright?"

"Yer, I had some professional help," I replied

As I was telling the story about what happened I drove back up the road towards the pedestrian crossing, and guess what? The lads were still trying to 'cross' the road safely!

# Sex

I got a pick up at the train station in Wigan town centre. It was about four o'clock in the morning as I pulled into the station and there was only one person waiting. She was about twenty two years of age, and drop dead gorgeous. She had on a very short skirt or it could have been a belt it was that short and she had a bingo top on, (eyes down). What I didn't notice was that she had no bag, mainly because my eyes were elsewhere. She got into the front seat next to me and told me her destination.

She started chatting away telling me that she lost her mates and that's why she was on her own. Half way through the journey she drops the bomb shell, "I've got no money."

I gave a little sigh, she knows and I know that I'm not going to kick a young girl out of the car in the middle of the night, but before I could say anything to her she turned and faced me and said "Is there another way I can sort the fare out with you?"

I turned my head to look at her, god she was gorgeous.

"What do you mean?" I asked.

"Come on do I have to spell it out?" she said.

"I think you'll have to," I replied.

She looked at me and gave out a little laugh, at which point I was starting to get annoyed, not only aren't I getting paid but she is now taking the piss out of me. She then smiled and said, "When we get back to mine, come in and I will let you do whatever you want to me."

The penny dropped, this drop dead gorgeous girl was offering me sex, I looked at her, I couldn't believe my luck, my heart was racing. Just the thought of being with this girl would be enough for most men's hearts to race a little but I was going to have sex with her. I looked at her again, 'I couldn't get a girl like this when I was twenty two, never mind forty two' I thought.

"Well?" she said, "are you coming back to mine?"

Just as I was about to answer her, I woke up, BECAUSE THIS DOESN'T FUCKING HAPPEN!!!!!!!!!!!!!!!!!! ........well not to me anyway!!!!!!!!!

# Some People You Have To Forgive

This taxi tale is about a 'spewer', this is what we call someone who is sick in the car, and again I think we put a lot of effort into coming up with this terminology.

Now over the last twenty years I've had about twenty to thirty people being sick in my car. It's not really something I actually keep count on, but this particular one really sticks in my mind. When someone is sick in a taxi there is a cleaning charge, which is anything up to fifty pounds.

It was on 26th March 1998 when this person was sick in my car, now you may be thinking 'god this guy holds a grudge remembering the date', well, the reason I remember this date is that I picked up my new car that day, well new to me, it was a three year old blue Vauxhall Vectra. You know what it's like getting a new car, the smell, everything shiny, trying to find out what all the buttons are for, I was like a big kid.

I drove from the car dealership to our taxi office, and when you get a new car you do tend to drive like Morgan Freeman out of Driving Miss Daisy. When I got to the taxi office, they fitted a taxi radio and a meter into the car; this took about hour and a half. When it was all ready for work and I stopped showing it off to other taxi drivers, off I went to pick up the first person to travel in my new car.

The passengers got into the car, one in the front and one in the back, again with my Morgan Freeman cap on I drove out of the road and turned left, one hundred yards up the road I came to a roundabout, turned left, and that's when I had my own version of The Exorcist. The person sitting in the front threw up everywhere, all over my new shiny dashboard, over the gear stick, over the carpet and also over themselves. I pulled over into a nearby bus stop and just sat there looking at the mess all over the place, 'my new car', I thought. I just couldn't believe it, I turned towards the passenger, who looked at me, and by the look in their eye they could tell I wasn't a happy bunny. Then my passenger opened their mouth and began to speak.

"I'm sorry daddy," my six year old daughter said to me, damn those heart strings!!!!!!!! I gave her a cuddle and drove her straight home, cleaned her up and then cleaned the car up.

My three year old daughter who was sitting in the back had great delight telling her mother about what just happened. What made her sick I don't know but a little bit of advice here, never give your child pickled onion crisps before you go on a journey, the smell was there for days.

Still to this day they laugh about it, and I still tell her that she owes me fifty pounds, to which she responds with a kiss on the cheek! I'm paying the bill off a kiss at a time. Who would have daughters?

# Why Did I Open My Mouth

On Saturday night I got a job to pick up at the Grafton night club in Liverpool. The Grafton is quite a well known nightclub, it's been going for about fifty years, even my mother used to go there when she was a teenager. The job was booked for 2am and I got there 5 minutes to two, pulled into the garage across the road from the Grafton and waited for my customer to arrive. Within minutes a young couple walked to my car, told me their name, and to my relief it was my fare.

They got into the car, the young girl told me were they wanted to go and off we went. I was going to try and start a conversation with them but as I looked into my rear view mirror, they were kissing the faces off each other, so I decided not to bother. Things went quiet in the back of my car, the guy had his head back on the head rest with his eyes closed, and I couldn't see her, so I assumed that she was going to sleep as well, how wrong, or rather naive, was I?

As we approached the Showcase cinema on the East Lancs road, the lad suddenly spoke.

"Hey mate," he said.

I nearly jumped out of my skin when the silence was broken. I looked at him through the rear view mirror, he had this big grin across his face.

"Guess what?" he said.

"What?" I asked, looking between the mirror and the road.

"I just had the best blow job ever," he said, with a smirk spreading wider and wider across his face.

I looked at him in disbelief and said, "Well I hope she fucking swallowed mate, because you'll be paying if there's any mess."

Before he could answer, the girl screamed, "STOP THIS FUCKING CAR!" and popped her head up suddenly from behind my seat. I looked at her in the mirror, she repeated in a louder, angrier and more pronounced voice, "I SAID STOP THIS FUCKING CAR!!"

I pulled over to the side of the road as soon as I could as I had determined from her tone it would be much better to do exactly what she instructed, and turned around to face them. The lad still had a huge fucking grin plastered all over his face, she however, didn't! She leaned across him and opened the door, "GET THE FUCK OUT OF THIS CAR RIGHT NOW DICKHEAD!!!!!!" she screamed at him.

I was just looking at them in disbelief, less than two minutes ago she was going down on him, now she was screaming at him to get out, but to be fair I could understand why........ well sort of!!!

He was still sat there, still with this stupid fucking grin on his face, and I really could understand why, not moving.

"GET THE FUCK OUT!!" she screamed once again.

At this point I myself was considering getting the 'FUCK' out as this was now an extremely scary woman!

He let out a huge satisfied sigh, still with the stupid grin.

"Aaagh fuck it! I only live a mile down the road from here," he said, then got out of the car, turned around to face the girl and calmly asked, "I suppose a shag is out of the question then darlin'?"

He then, not waiting or, I doubt even expecting an answer, casually swaggered away. To my horror I found myself biting my lip in order not to laugh, because firstly I didn't like him so did not want him knowing I thought his question, after everything, was funny, and secondly, I did not want to become the target of the woman's wrath.

"JUST FUCK OFF!!!" she screamed again as she slammed the back door. 'What has the door done to deserve that' I thought, as I often did when the door had been targeted in anger.

The now bravado consumed lad just laughed and walked away. After a short and rather thoughtful pause, I regained my composure and continued with the 'taxi driving'! It was a very quiet journey. We got to her destination and she paid me, and walked into her house.

I drove around the corner, stopped the car to check if there was any mess and to my relief there wasn't.

'Good girl.' I thought! ................. Strangely enough, I still to this very day remember her exact address!!!!!!!!!!!!!!!!!!

# The Weather must be Really Bad

Got a job from a local factory some years ago, to pick a business man up and take him to the airport. He was a tall man wearing an expensive looking suit and carrying a smart black briefcase.

He got in and in a strong German accent said, "Manchester Airport please."

"Ok, no problem," I replied.

We then set off up the dual-carriageway towards the motorway. The sky suddenly darkened and spots of rain began to fall, which soon got heavier and heavier until it was absolutely pouring down. I had to adjust my heater vents and face the warm air at my windscreen and had my wipers going ten to the dozen in order to see where I was going.

After about a mile travelling in silence, the man leaned forwards and peered up towards the ominous thunder clouds. He gazed for a few seconds then sat back in his chair. He shook his head and then said, "Why oh why we ever wanted to invade this country is completely beyond me!"

How apt, a German in England with a cracking sense of humour!

# It's Not What You Know, It's Who You Know

Many years ago whilst working for Ormskirk Taxis, I was given a job at an address in Aughton. I found the house and pulled into the gravel driveway. The house was huge and outside there were expensive luxury cars parked. A man and a woman came out, both dressed to the nines, and got in my car.

"Where to mate?" I asked

"Erm, can you take us to the Masonic Hall in Liverpool please?" the man asked.

"Yer no problem mate," I said, and backed out of the driveway.

"We're running a bit late, so if you can could you put your foot down a bit?" the man asked.

"I'll do my best mate," I told him.

"Ok, thank you," he said.

The journey began, through some winding country roads, and then onto the long A59 towards Liverpool, where I could at last 'put my foot down'. The road was very empty, and the several sets of traffic lights were kind and stayed on green as we sped along.

As I approached them, the lights at Maghull Square, were also green. As I got nearer they changed to amber. I was so close I hesitated slightly, then decided to go through, as stopping would have taken me over the line and actually through the lights anyway, which would have left me blocking the junction.

The lights then changed to red as my front wheels crossed the line and as I continued through I noticed on my right, a Police car. He decided not to turn right, but in fact do a U turn and follow me.

I slowed slightly down and watched as he quickly caught up to me, blue lights flashing. He pulled up alongside of me at the next lights that I had to stop at and pointed towards a bus stop further on, and shouted through his open passenger's window, to me, "Pull up in that bus stop!" he ordered.

The lights changed to green, and I drove to the bus stop and pulled in.

"Everything ok?" the man behind me asked.

"I'll soon find out," I told him, and got out of my car.

The police car parked behind me, and the officer emerged, stern faced and already opening his ticket book.

"Do you know why I've stopped you?" He asked looking at his ticket book.

"No," I replied.

"So you drove through a red light and didn't notice then?"

"I didn't, I drove through an amber light," I pointed out.

"Even if that was the case sir, an amber light means stop," he said, still looking at his ticket book.

"Yes it does, but only if it is safe to do so. As there was a car close behind me, and I was right on top of the lights, I decided that attempting to stop so quickly would have been hazardous for the car behind and would have left me in the middle of the junction and through the lights when I came to a halt. So the safest option was to continue through," I explained.

"I see. So can you tell me what the next sequence was in the four sets of traffic lights?" he asked.

"I assume that the lights you were stopped at would have signaled you to turn right," I guessed.

"Correct. I'm surprised that you even noticed me considering the speed you were going sir!"

"As I said, I took everything into consideration as my decision to choose the safest option was made. If I had chosen to stop, you would have been blocked from turning right as my car would have been in the middle of the junction."

"So is this your car sir?" he asked, ignoring my explanation.

"Yes" I answered.

He glanced at my car, then said, "So, you're a professional driver then I see, right then, I'm going to write you an on the spot fine, which also carries a three point penalty endorsement on your driving license. I'll do you a favour though, and won't mention the fact you drove through a red light, I'll do you for speeding, as the main offence is much more serious. As you earn you living from driving I'm happy to deal with this matter in this way ok?"

There was nothing I could say or do to change his mind, so I simply nodded in agreement.

He then began writing out the ticket, taking details from my number plate and my taxi plate. As he did this, the smartly dressed man in the back of my car turned and looked at him. The officer looked up at him, and the man smiled, then nodded at him. The officer suddenly stopped writing, nodded back at the man and then, to my utter astonishment, he tore the almost completed ticket from the book, screwed it up and put it in his pocket. He then closed the book and turned to face me.

"Right," he started, "I've decided to let you off with a warning on this occasion sir, so I suggest that you slow down, and approach traffic lights with more caution. I think I've kept you and your passengers long enough sir, now, you be on your way, and remember drive safely sir."

With that he got back into the police car and drove away. I was stunned. I'd heard several stories regarding 'The Masons' but until now, had never thought they were actually true.

I got back into my car and continued the drive to the Masonic Hall. After about a mile the man behind me spoke.

"Is everything ok? Did he give you a ticket?" he asked.

"Err, no, he didn't, he was going to but, suddenly changed his mind." I told him.

"That was lucky then, wasn't it?" he asked.

"Lucky? I didn't know about that mate. He changed his mind when he saw you, that's what happened," I explained.

"Me? What do you mean? Why would he change his mind after seeing me?"

"I don't know really, maybe it was because he noticed you had a nipple poking out of your shirt and one leg of your trousers rolled up!" I said.

The paused, then suddenly roared with laughter. When I had picked the man and his partner up, I already knew he was a grandmaster of some lodge, and was quite aware that many police officers were also Masons and that they abided by many things including a 'you scratch my back and I'll scratch yours' policy towards fellow masons.

To witness this first hand just confirmed my belief, still I was thankful for the outcome of my meeting of masons that seemingly 'scratched each other'.

# The Office

Here are some short stories from the people who answer the phones in the taxi office I work for. These are actual calls and do make you wonder how some people survive in life.

The first story was at Christmas time, this and New Years eve are the only times of year that we put our fares up, we charge double time.

RING RING.............

Office, "Evening taxi's."

Customer, "Hello, what rate are you charging on Christmas day?"

Office, "Its double time."

Customer, "Well my fare is normally £4, how much will that be on double time?"

Office, "Erm... Just a second, I'll work that out for you.... Right, 4 plus 4 equals erm, eight, so that would be £8."

Customer, "And my fare for the journey home is £4 how much will that be?"

Office, "I'll just calculate that for you too, right so 4 plus 4 would again equal eight I think, so erm, that would also be £8."

Customer, "Ok thanks for your help goodbye"

Office, "Bye"........ 'God it's going to be a long night.'

Approximately twenty minutes later that same evening.............

RING RING

Office, "Hello taxis"

Customer, "Hello, you couldn't do us a favour could you?"

Office, "That would depend on what exactly the favour is."

Customer, "Could you tell the taxi driver who is watching me and my boyfriend having sex, to stop watching us please?"

Office, "Erm…. yer ok, consider it done!"

Customer, "Thank you, bye."

Office, "Ok bye now."


Even later that same evening........................

RING RING

Office, "Taxis"

Customer, "What's the rate on New Year's Eve?"

Office, "Its double time."

Customer, "How much will it be to Liverpool?"

Office "It's about £40."

Customer, "There and back?"

Office, "No, sorry that's one way, it would be about £80 there and back."

Customer, "Would any of your drivers do it for £10?"

Customer, "Hello?"

Office, "Yer sorry still here, you want us to take you to Liverpool for £10 when it would cost £40?"

Customer, "No I want you to take me there and back for £10."

Office, "Sorry but you've got no chance."

Customer, "I'm a single parent and can't afford taxi fares."

Office, "Well why are you ringing a taxi firm then?"

Customer, "Because I need to go out on New Year's Eve, and I haven't been out all year."

Office, "We picked you up last week from the pub."

Customer, "Are you going to do it or what?"

Office, "No!"

Customer, "I'm going to report you for being prejudice towards single parents."

Phone goes dead

7 hours to go!!!

# Coming in October 2013

# The Next

# Philip Parry

# Novel

# Wishful Thinking...2

Allan is granted 3 wishes and he 'knows' he is, and eventually after a lot of doubt decides to test this out by making a 'wish'. His wish to his utter astonishment is granted!!!!!! Allan now has an almighty power at his disposal, the question is 'how' will he use it????????????

# Also

# Coming later this year

# View From My Mind 3

Philip Parry's, third collection of poetry in my 'View From' series.

Please visit my webpage http://philipparry.weebly.com/